THE EUGÉNIE ROCHEROLLE SERIES

Intermediate Piano Solo/Duet

Fantasia del Tango

6 Original Piano Solos and 1 Duet by Eugénie Rocherolle

To my good friend and colleague Kathleen A. Theisen,
with deep appreciation for her support over the years.

PLAYBACK+
Speed • Pitch • Balance • Loop

To access audio, visit:
www.halleonard.com/mylibrary

Enter Code
4471-2751-2288-7159

ISBN 978-1-4950-7783-8

7777 W. BLUEMOUND RD. P.O. BOX 13819 MILWAUKEE, WI 53213

In Australia Contact:
Hal Leonard Australia Pty. Ltd.
4 Lentara Court
Cheltenham, Victoria, 3192 Australia
Email: ausadmin@halleonard.com.au

Visit Hal Leonard Online at
www.halleonard.com

FROM THE COMPOSER

The tango is Argentina's contribution to the world of dance. Believed to have originated in the poorer sections of Buenos Aires, it began to change in the late 1800's with the arrival of European immigrants. They brought with them their music and dances which, when combined with those of Argentina, gave us what is known as the Argentine Tango, the "dance of the heart."

Originally performed by men (solo or a pair) to attract the ladies, eventually the male-female couple became the norm. This brought more excitement and appeal and quickly spread throughout the continents where it remains one of the most popular world music genres.

Eugénie

Eugénie Rocherolle
December 2016

CONTENTS

DEBAJO LAS ESTRELLAS
(Under the Stars)

EUGÉNIE ROCHEROLLE

Allegro moderato (♩ = 132)

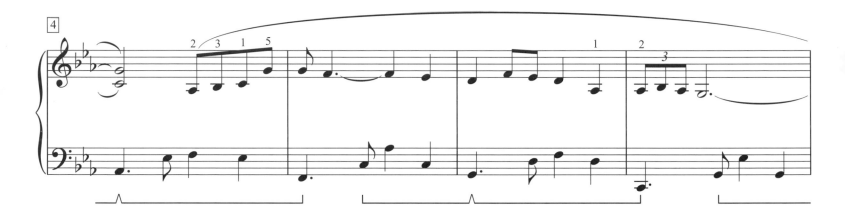

5

5

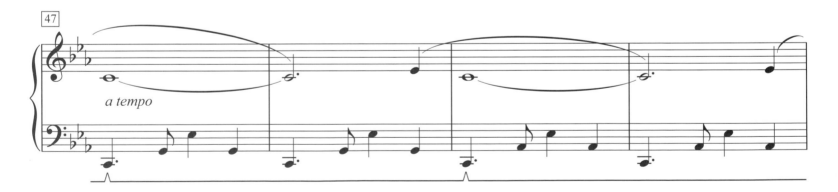

OJOS DE COQUETA
(Teasing Eyes)

EUGÉNIE ROCHEROLLE

Allegro moderato (♩ = 126)

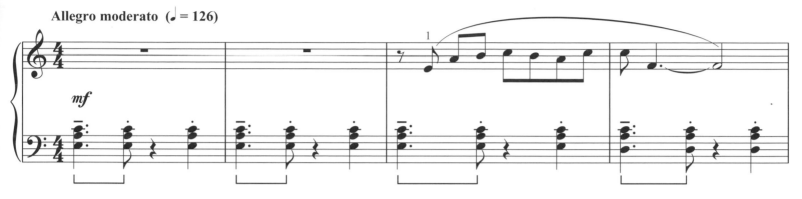

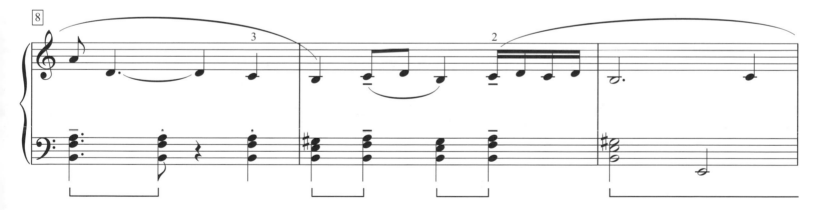

8

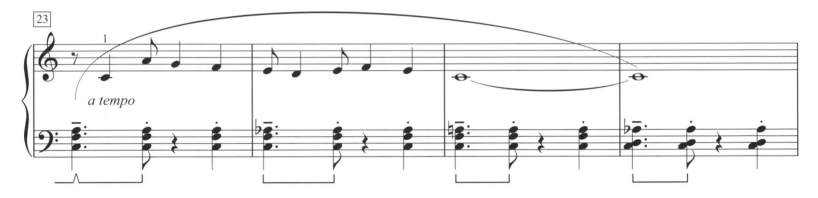

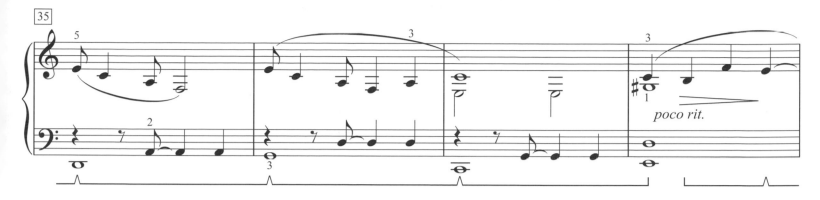

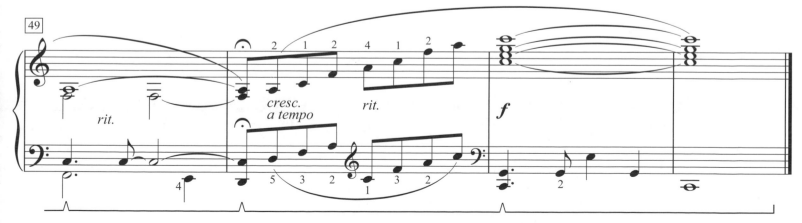

PROMESA DE AMOR
(Promise of Love)

EUGÉNIE ROCHEROLLE

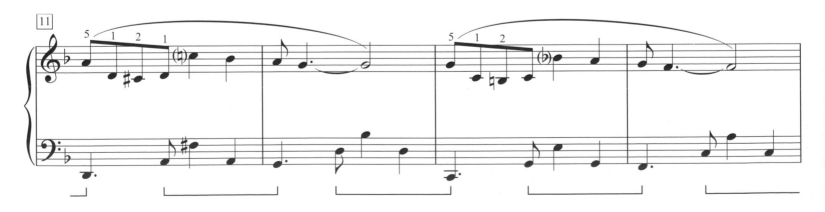

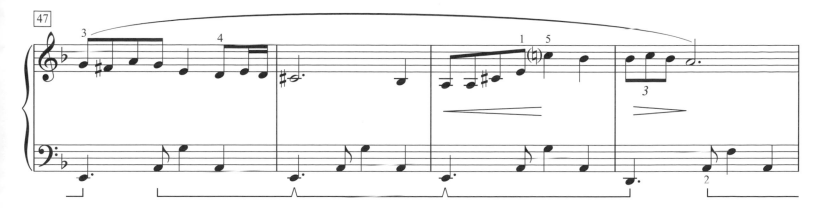

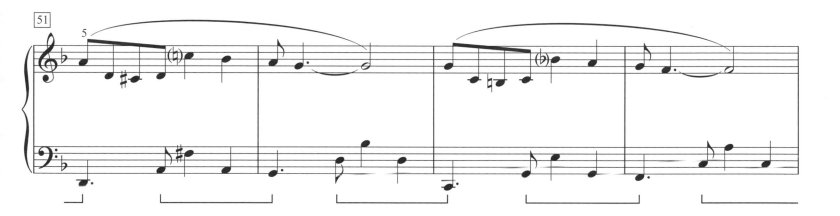

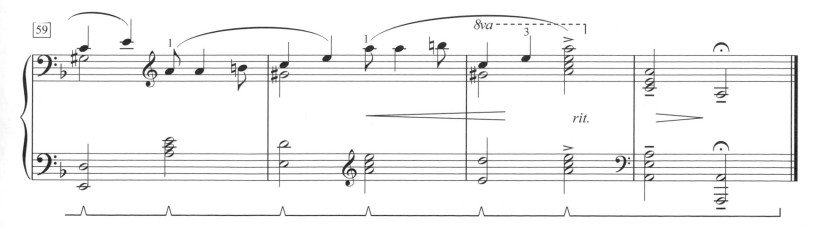

SUEÑOS DE TI
(Dreams of You)

EUGÉNIE ROCHEROLLE

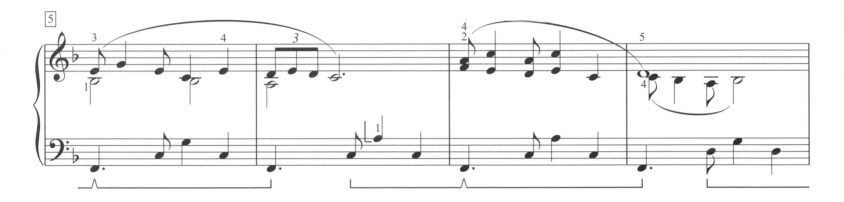

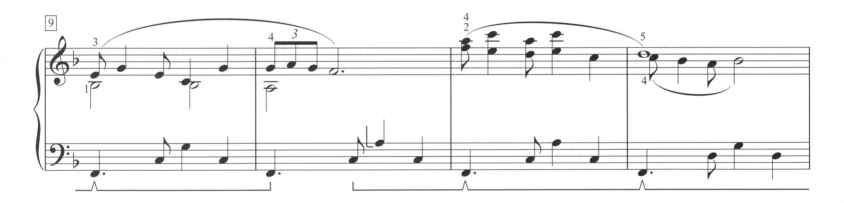

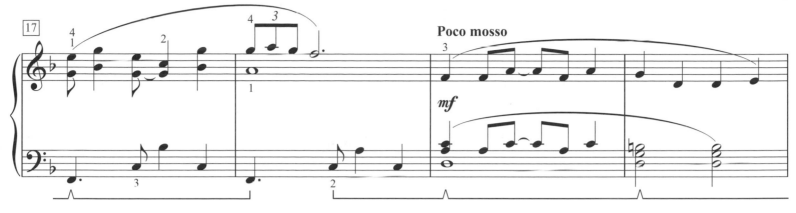

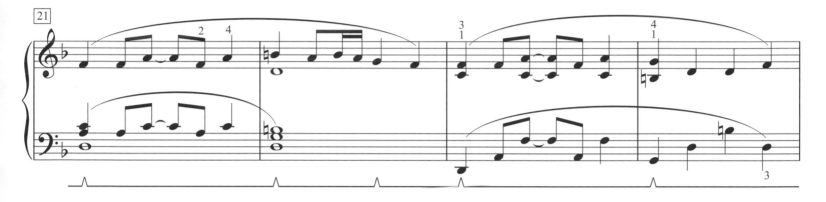

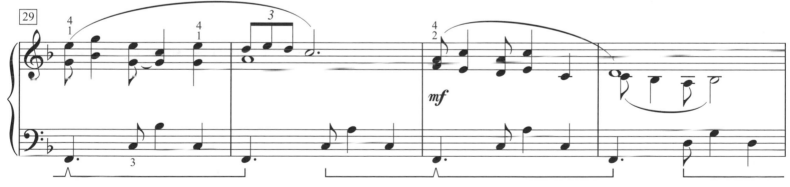

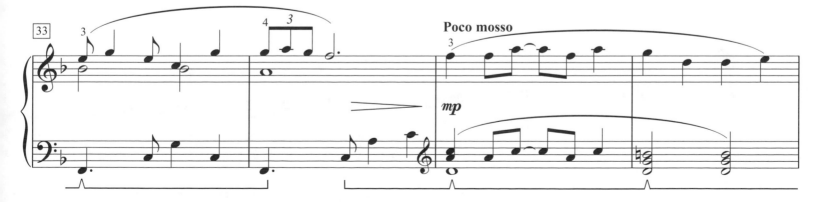

15

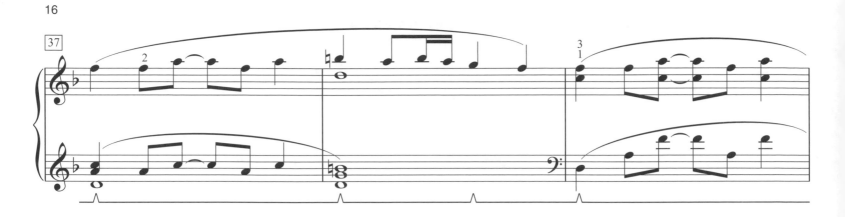

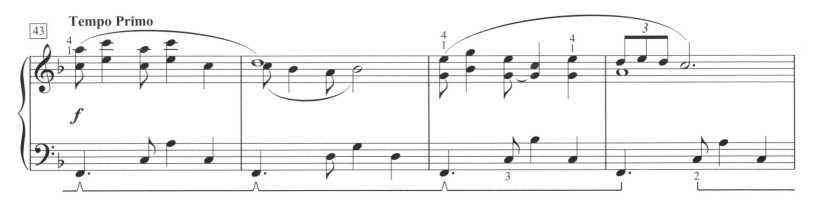

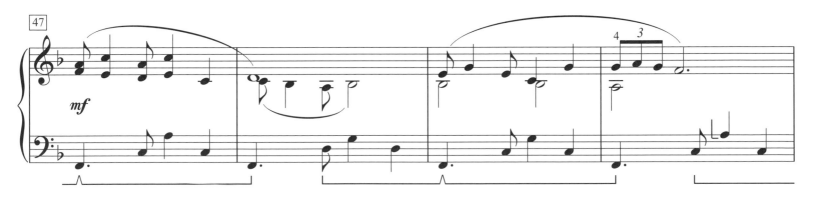

SUSPIROS
(Longings)

EUGÉNIE ROCHEROLLE

Allegro moderato (♩ = 120)

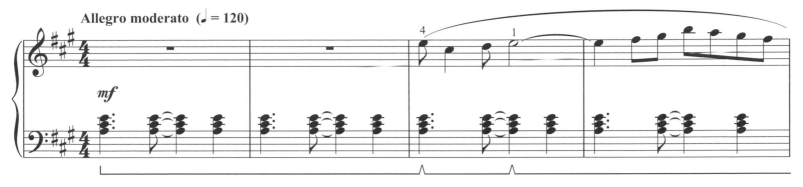

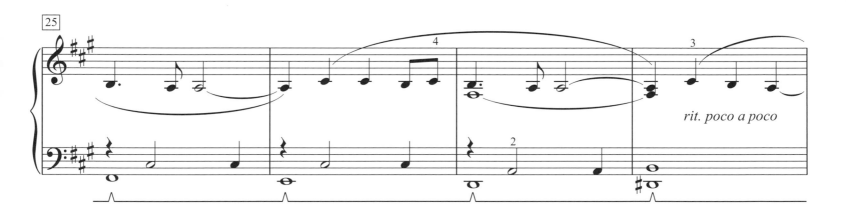

TANGO CAPRICHOSO
(Tango Fancy)

EUGÉNIE ROCHEROLLE

* pedal on beat 2

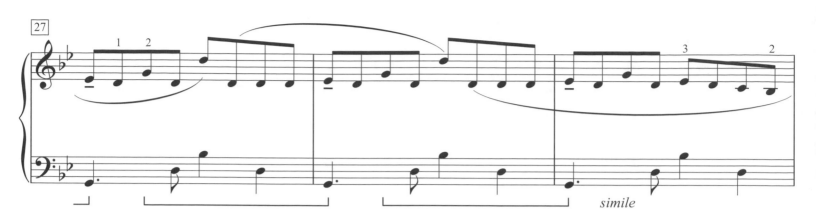

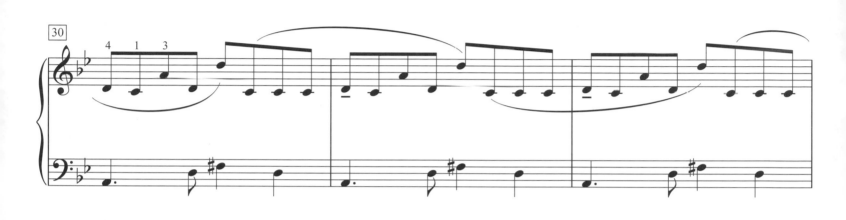

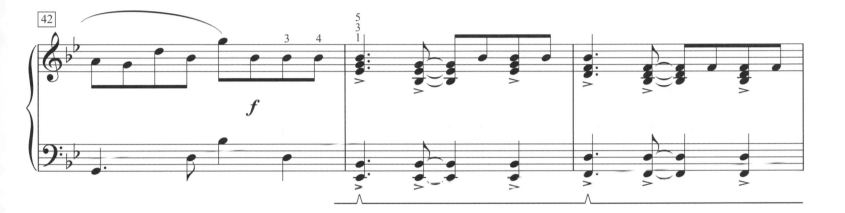

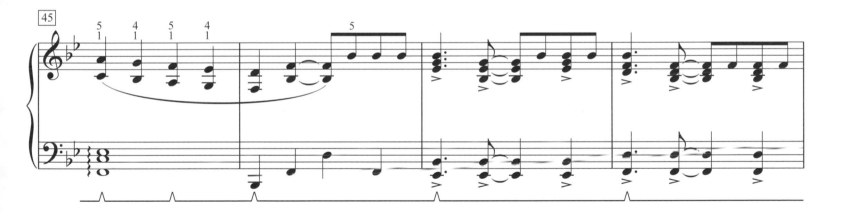

BAILANDO CONMIGO
(Dancing with Me)

EUGÉNIE ROCHEROLLE

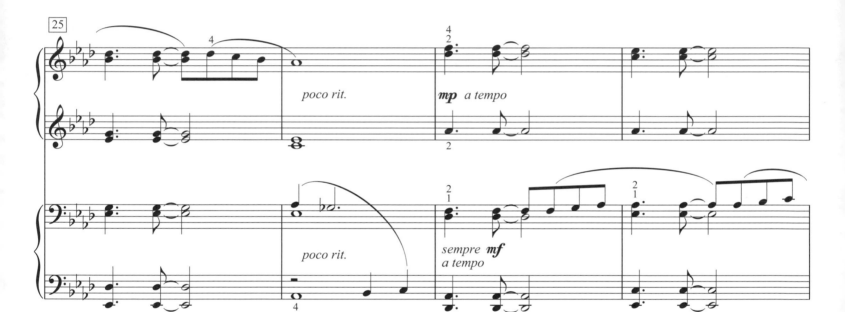

Piano for Two

A VARIETY OF PIANO DUETS FROM HAL LEONARD

ADELE FOR PIANO DUET

Eight of Adele's biggest hits arranged especially for intermediate piano duet! Featuring: Chasing Pavements • Hello • Make You Feel My Love • Rolling in the Deep • Set Fire to the Rain • Skyfall • Someone Like You • When We Were Young.

00172162..................$14.99

CONTEMPORARY DISNEY DUETS

8 Disney piano duets to play and perform with a friend! Includes: Almost There • He's a Pirate • I See the Light • Let It Go • Married Life • That's How You Know • Touch the Sky • We Belong Together.

00128259 ....$12.99

BILLY JOEL FOR PIANO DUET

Includes 8 of the Piano Man's greatest hits. Perfect as recital encores, or just for fun! Titles: Just the Way You Are • The Longest Time • My Life • Piano Man • She's Always a Woman • Uptown Girl • and more.

00141139 ....$14.99

THE BEATLES PIANO DUETS – 2ND EDITION

Features 8 arrangements: Can't Buy Me Love • Eleanor Rigby • Hey Jude • Let It Be • Penny Lane • Something • When I'm Sixty-Four • Yesterday.

00290496..................$15.99

EASY CLASSICAL DUETS

7 great piano duets to perform at a recital, play-for-fun, or sightread! Titles: By the Beautiful Blue Danube (Strauss) • Eine kleine Nachtmusik (Mozart) • Sleeping Beauty Waltz (Tchaikovsky) • and more.

00145767 Book/Online Audio $10.99

RHAPSODY IN BLUE FOR PIANO DUET

George Gershwin
Arranged by Brent Edstrom
This intimate adaptation delivers access to advancing pianists and provides an exciting musical collaboration and adventure!

00125150 ....$12.99

CHART HITS FOR EASY DUET

10 great early intermediate pop duets! Play with a friend or with the online audio: All of Me • Grenade • Happy • Hello • Just Give Me a Reason • Roar • Shake It Off • Stay • Stay with Me • Thinking Out Loud.

00159796 Book/Online Audio $12.99

THE SOUND OF MUSIC

9 arrangements from the movie/musical, including: Do-Re-Mi • Edelweiss • Maria • My Favorite Things • So Long, Farewell • The Sound of Music • and more.

00290389..................$14.99

RIVER FLOWS IN YOU AND OTHER SONGS ARRANGED FOR PIANO DUET

10 great songs arranged for 1 piano, 4 hands, including the title song and: All of Me (Piano Guys) • Bella's Lullaby • Beyond • Chariots of Fire • Dawn • Forrest Gump - Main Title (Feather Theme) • Primavera • Somewhere in Time • Watermark.

00141055 ....$12.99

STAR WARS

8 intergalactic arrangements of *Star Wars* themes for late intermediate to early advanced piano duet, including: Across the Stars • Cantina Band • Duel of the Fates • The Imperial March (Darth Vader's Theme) • Princess Leia's Theme • Star Wars (Main Theme) • The Throne Room (And End Title) • Yoda's Theme.

00119405..................$14.99

HAL LEONARD PIANO DUET PLAY-ALONG SERIES

This great series comes with audio that features separate tracks for the Primo and Secondo parts – perfect for practice and performance! Visit www.halleonard.com for a complete list of titles in the series!

COLDPLAY

Clocks • Paradise • The Scientist • A Sky Full of Stars • Speed of Sound • Trouble • Viva La Vida • Yellow.
00141054..................$14.99

FROZEN

Do You Want to Build a Snowman? • Fixer Upper • For the First Time in Forever • In Summer • Let It Go • Love Is an Open Door • Reindeer(s) Are Better Than People.
00128260..................$14.99

JAZZ STANDARDS

All the Things You Are • Bewitched • Cheek to Cheek • Don't Get Around Much Anymore • Georgia on My Mind • In the Mood • It's Only a Paper Moon • Satin Doll • The Way You Look Tonight.
00290577..................$14.99

www.halleonard.com

COMPOSER SHOWCASE
HAL LEONARD STUDENT PIANO LIBRARY

This series showcases great original piano music from our **Hal Leonard Student Piano Library** family of composers. Carefully graded for easy selection.

BILL BOYD

JAZZ BITS (AND PIECES)
Early Intermediate Level
00290312 11 Solos..............$7.99

JAZZ DELIGHTS
Intermediate Level
00240435 11 Solos..............$8.99

JAZZ FEST
Intermediate Level
00240436 10 Solos..............$8.99

JAZZ PRELIMS
Early Elementary Level
00290032 12 Solos..............$7.99

JAZZ SKETCHES
Intermediate Level
00220001 8 Solos..............$8.99

JAZZ STARTERS
Elementary Level
00290425 10 Solos..............$8.99

JAZZ STARTERS II
Late Elementary Level
00290434 11 Solos..............$7.99

JAZZ STARTERS III
Late Elementary Level
00290465 12 Solos..............$8.99

THINK JAZZ!
Early Intermediate Level
00290417 Method Book..........$12.99

TONY CARAMIA

JAZZ MOODS
Intermediate Level
00296728 8 Solos..............$6.95

SUITE DREAMS
Intermediate Level
00296775 4 Solos..............$6.99

SONDRA CLARK

DAKOTA DAYS
Intermediate Level
00296521 5 Solos..............$6.95

FLORIDA FANTASY SUITE
Intermediate Level
00296766 3 Duets..............$7.95

THREE ODD METERS
Intermediate Level
00296472 3 Duets..............$6.95

MATTHEW EDWARDS

CONCERTO FOR YOUNG PIANISTS
FOR 2 PIANOS, FOUR HANDS
Intermediate Level Book/CD
00296356 3 Movements $19.99

CONCERTO NO. 2 IN G MAJOR
FOR 2 PIANOS, 4 HANDS
Intermediate Level Book/CD
00296670 3 Movements............$17.99

PHILLIP KEVEREN

MOUSE ON A MIRROR
Late Elementary Level
00296361 5 Solos..............$8.99

MUSICAL MOODS
Elementary/Late Elementary Level
00296714 7 Solos..............$6.99

SHIFTY-EYED BLUES
Late Elementary Level
00296374 5 Solos..............$7.99

CAROL KLOSE

THE BEST OF CAROL KLOSE
Early to Late Intermediate Level
00146151 15 Solos..............$12.99

CORAL REEF SUITE
Late Elementary Level
00296354 7 Solos..............$7.50

DESERT SUITE
Intermediate Level
00296667 6 Solos..............$7.99

FANCIFUL WALTZES
Early Intermediate Level
00296473 5 Solos..............$7.95

GARDEN TREASURES
Late Intermediate Level
00296787 5 Solos..............$8.50

ROMANTIC EXPRESSIONS
Intermediate to Late Intermediate Level
00296923 5 Solos..............$8.99

WATERCOLOR MINIATURES
Early Intermediate Level
00296848 7 Solos..............$7.99

JENNIFER LINN

AMERICAN IMPRESSIONS
Intermediate Level
00296471 6 Solos..............$8.99

ANIMALS HAVE FEELINGS TOO
Early Elementary/Elementary Level
00147789 8 Solos..............$8.99

AU CHOCOLAT
Late Elementary/Early Intermediate Level
00298110 7 Solos..............$8.99

CHRISTMAS IMPRESSIONS
Intermediate Level
00296706 8 Solos..............$8.99

JUST PINK
Elementary Level
00296722 9 Solos..............$8.99

LES PETITES IMAGES
Late Elementary Level
00296664 7 Solos..............$8.99

LES PETITES IMPRESSIONS
Intermediate Level
00296355 6 Solos..............$8.99

REFLECTIONS
Late Intermediate Level
00296843 5 Solos..............$8.99

TALES OF MYSTERY
Intermediate Level
00296769 6 Solos..............$8.99

LYNDA LYBECK-ROBINSON

ALASKA SKETCHES
Early Intermediate Level
00119637 8 Solos..............$8.99

AN AWESOME ADVENTURE
Late Elementary Level
00137563 8 Solos..............$7.99

FOR THE BIRDS
Early Intermediate/Intermediate Level
00237078 9 Solos..............$8.99

WHISPERING WOODS
Late Elementary Level
00275905 9 Solos..............$8.99

MONA REJINO

CIRCUS SUITE
Late Elementary Level
00296665 5 Solos..............$8.99

COLOR WHEEL
Early Intermediate Level
00201951 6 Solos..............$9.99

IMPRESIONES DE ESPAÑA
Intermediate Level
00337520 6 Solos..............$8.99

IMPRESSIONS OF NEW YORK
Intermediate Level
00364212..............$8.99

JUST FOR KIDS
Elementary Level
00296840 8 Solos..............$7.99

MERRY CHRISTMAS MEDLEYS
Intermediate Level
00296799 5 Solos..............$8.99

MINIATURES IN STYLE
Intermediate Level
00148088 6 Solos..............$8.99

PORTRAITS IN STYLE
Early Intermediate Level
00296507 6 Solos..............$8.99

EUGÉNIE ROCHEROLLE

CELEBRATION SUITE
Intermediate Level
00152724 3 Duets..............$8.99

ENCANTOS ESPAÑOLES (SPANISH DELIGHTS)
Intermediate Level
00125451 6 Solos..............$8.99

JAMBALAYA
Intermediate Level
00296654 2 Pianos, 8 Hands.....$12.99
00296725 2 Pianos, 4 Hands.......$7.95

JEROME KERN CLASSICS
Intermediate Level
00296577 10 Solos..............$12.99

LITTLE BLUES CONCERTO
Early Intermediate Level
00142801 2 Pianos, 4 Hands......$12.99

TOUR FOR TWO
Late Intermediate Level
00296832 6 Duets..............$9.99

TREASURES
Late Elementary/Early Intermediate Level
00296924 7 Solos..............$8.99

JEREMY SISKIND

BIG APPLE JAZZ
Intermediate Level
00278209 8 Solos..............$8.99

MYTHS AND MONSTERS
Late Elementary/Early Intermediate Level
00148148 9 Solos..............$8.99

CHRISTOS TSITSAROS

DANCES FROM AROUND THE WORLD
Early Intermediate Level
00296688 7 Solos..............$8.99

FIVE SUMMER PIECES
Late Intermediate/Advanced Level
00361235 5 Solos..............$12.99

LYRIC BALLADS
Intermediate/Late Intermediate Level
00102404 6 Solos..............$8.99

POETIC MOMENTS
Intermediate Level
00296403 8 Solos..............$8.99

SEA DIARY
Early Intermediate Level
00253186 9 Solos..............$8.99

SONATINA HUMORESQUE
Late Intermediate Level
00296772 3 Movements..............$6.99

SONGS WITHOUT WORDS
Intermediate Level
00296506 9 Solos..............$9.99

THREE PRELUDES
Early Advanced Level
00130747 3 Solos..............$8.99

THROUGHOUT THE YEAR
Late Elementary Level
00296723 12 Duets..............$6.95

ADDITIONAL COLLECTIONS

AT THE LAKE
by Elvina Pearce
Elementary/Late Elementary Level
00131642 10 Solos and Duets.....$7.99

CHRISTMAS FOR TWO
by Dan Fox
Early Intermediate Level
00290069 13 Duets..............$8.99

CHRISTMAS JAZZ
by Mike Springer
Intermediate Level
00296525 6 Solos..............$8.99

COUNTY RAGTIME FESTIVAL
by Fred Kern
Intermediate Level
00296882 7 Solos..............$7.99

LITTLE JAZZERS
by Jennifer Watts
Elementary/Late Elementary Level
00154573 9 Solos..............$8.99

PLAY THE BLUES!
by Luann Carman
Early Intermediate Level
00296357 10 Solos..............$9.99

ROLLER COASTERS & RIDES
by Jennifer & Mike Watts
Intermediate Level
00131144 8 Duets..............$8.99

www.halleonard.com

Prices, contents, and availability subject to change without notice.

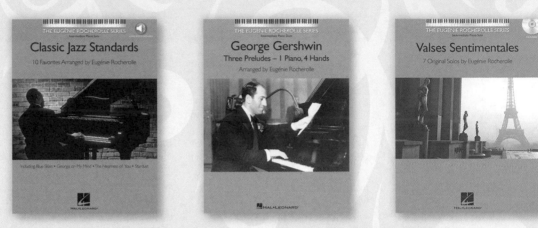